CELEBRATING THE CITY OF TORONTO

Celebrating the City of Toronto

Walter the Educator

Silent King Books

SILENT KING BOOKS

SKB

Copyright © 2024 by Walter the Educator

All rights reserved. No part of this book may be reproduced in any manner whatsoever without written permission except in the case of brief quotations embodied in critical articles and reviews.

First Printing, 2024

Disclaimer
This book is a literary work; the story is not about specific persons, locations, situations, and/or circumstances unless mentioned in a historical context. Any resemblance to real persons, locations, situations, and/or circumstances is coincidental. This book is for entertainment and informational purposes only. The author and publisher offer this information without warranties expressed or implied. No matter the grounds, neither the author nor the publisher will be accountable for any losses, injuries, or other damages caused by the reader's use of this book. The use of this book acknowledges an understanding and acceptance of this disclaimer.

Celebrating the City of Toronto is a little collectible souvenir book that belongs to the Celebrating Cities Book Series by Walter the Educator. Collect them all and more books at WaltertheEducator.com
USE THE EXTRA SPACE TO TAKE NOTES AND DOCUMENT YOUR MEMORIES

TORONTO

In the heart of Canada, where the maple leaves sway,

Celebrating the City of
Toronto

Lies Toronto, a city where dreams weave and play.

Rising towers of glass reach for the sky,

Reflecting the hues of a sunset's soft sigh.

A mosaic of cultures, a vibrant parade,

In Kensington Market, where histories fade.

The aromas of spices, the tapestry grand,

Each corner, a new world, each street a new land.

By the lakeside, serene, where the gulls freely soar,

Celebrating the City of Toronto

Lies the echo of legends, of tales from the shore.

From the whispers of Haudenosaunee lore,

To the murmurs of traders in times of yore.

The CN Tower, a sentinel proud,

Pierces the heavens, dispels every cloud.

A marvel of modernity, a beacon of light,

Guiding the city through day and through night.

In the Distillery District, where cobblestones gleam,

Past and present entwine in a seamless dream.

Artisans craft and musicians play,

In a timeless dance, night into day.

Celebrating the City of
Toronto

The hum of the city, a symphony grand,

From Bloor to the Beaches, where the waves kiss the sand.

St. Lawrence Market, a treasure chest bright,

Where flavors and stories converge in delight.

Streetcars trundle through the arteries vast,

Connecting the present to echoes of past.

From Queen Street's pulse to Yonge's vibrant beat,

Toronto's rhythm is felt in each street.

In High Park's embrace, where blossoms unfold,

Celebrating the City of
Toronto

Nature and nurture in harmony bold.

Cherry trees whisper secrets in bloom,

As joggers and dreamers find solace from gloom.

The lights of Dundas, a carnival's flair,

Where the world's many faces find laughter to share.

Eaton Centre's bustle, a shopper's delight,

Where dreams are envisioned, in day or in night.

Libraries that whisper the wisdom of ages,

The ROM and the AGO, cultural stages.

Exhibits and artifacts, stories untold,

Celebrating the City of
Toronto

In the halls of knowledge, the spirit is bold.

To Toronto, a jewel so bright,

In the tapestry of nations, a guiding light.

A city where stories and dreams intertwine,

In the heart of the True North, a treasure divine.

Celebrating the City of
Toronto

ABOUT THE CREATOR

Walter the Educator is one of the pseudonyms for Walter Anderson. Formally educated in Chemistry, Business, and Education, he is an educator, an author, a diverse entrepreneur, and he is the son of a disabled war veteran. "Walter the Educator" shares his time between educating and creating. He holds interests and owns several creative projects that entertain, enlighten, enhance, and educate, hoping to inspire and motivate you. Follow, find new works, and stay up to date with
Walter the Educator™ at
WaltertheEducator.com.

www.ingramcontent.com/pod-product-compliance
Lightning Source LLC
LaVergne TN
LVHW012048070526
838201LV00082B/3862